Written with Love
for

Nylah-May Shayne Service
&
XI-Ana Ray Service

From Mummy

This book belongs to:

Place your photo
here!

www.fast-print.net/store.php

The Beautiful Me Collection: When I Grow Up
Copyright © Marlene Service 2014

A catalogue record for this book is available from the British Library

ISBN 978-178456-094-2

An environmentally friendly book printed and bound in England by
www.printondemand-worldwide.com

Mixed Sources
Product group from well-managed
forests, and other controlled sources
www.fsc.org Cert no. TT-COC-002641
© 1996 Forest Stewardship Council
FSC

PEFC Certified
This product is
from sustainably
managed forests
and controlled
sources
www.pefc.org
PEFC
PEFC/16-33-415

This book is made entirely of chain-of-custody materials

This edition published 2014 by
Fastprint Publishing of Peterborough, England.

When I grow UP!

·The Beautiful Me·
·collection·

by Marlene Service

illustrated by Yuliya Yanishevska

Chef

I like to eat, I like to cook,
I've learnt all I know
From a recipe book.
Dinner and puddings are tasty to me,
My favourite is
Macaroni and Cheese.
I'm going to be a chef when I grow up.
I'm clever, I'm smart,
And I listen lots too,
So I can be anything,
And so can you.

Construction Worker

I'm going to be
a construction worker one day.
I like to drill,
I make lots of noise,
I will have tools,
But for now I've got toys.
I'm a good climber,
And I am very strong,
On a building site is where I belong.
I'm clever, I'm smart,
And I listen lots too,
So I can be anything,
And so can you.

Doctor

I'm going to be a doctor when I grow up.
I am caring,
I know just what to do.
You may have chicken pox,
You may have the flu,
You don't have to worry,
I'll come through,
Ill fix you up as good as new.
I'm patient,
I'm gentle,
I'm friendly,
I'm nice,
I'm clever, I'm smart,
And I listen lots too,
So I can be anything,
And so can you.

Fire Fighter

I'm going to be
a fireman when I grow up.
Just call for my help if you are in trouble,
You can count on me
I'll be there on the double.
I can sort things out no matter the task,
I am brave, I am strong,
I am quick, I am fast,
I'm clever, I'm smart,
And I listen lots too,
So I can be anything,
And so can you.

Musician

When I grow up
I'll be a musician,
I'll play wonderful music,
For you to listen.
I will practice and practice,
And maybe one day,
I'll get to play on a very big stage.
I'm clever, I'm smart,
And I listen lots too
So I can be anything,
And so can you.

Pilot

I love to travel,
I love to fly,
I really do,
I don't know why.
Amongst the clouds way up high,
I'll fly my plane across the sky.
I'd like to be a pilot
when I grow up.
I'm clever, I'm smart
And I listen lots too
So I can be anything,
And so can you.

Gymnast

I can flip, I can jump,
I can stretch out long and tall,
I can curl up like a hedgehog,
Into a small, tight ball,
I am quick, I am flexible,
I eat my fruits and vegetables.
I am clever, I am smart,
And I listen lots too,
So I can be anything,
And so can you.

Mechanic

On your old bike,
I can make the bolts tight,
On your old cars,
I can fit new parts.
I am good with metal,
I am good with steel,
If you get a puncture,
I'll replace your wheel.
Vans, trucks, lorries,
You don't have to worry,
I can help you out,
Just give me a shout.
I'm clever, I'm smart
And I listen lots too
So I can be anything,
And so can you.

Photographer

I'm going to be a photographer
When I grow up.
Snap snap snap.
Can I take your picture?
It doesn't matter what mood you're in,
I'll be sure to capture your grin.
You may be large,
You may be tall,
You may be big,
You may be small.
You can hang my pictures
Upon your wall.
I'm clever, I'm smart,
I listen lots too,
So I can be anything,
And so can you.

Graduate

When I'm big
I'm going to be a graduate.
I absolutely love to read,
Books are very interesting indeed.
I love to learn,
I like to write,
It doesn't matter day or night.
I'm clever, I'm smart,
And I listen lots too
So I can be anything
And so can you.

Builder

When I grow up I'm going to be a builder.
Bang bang bang!
I can drill,
I can build,
I can fix,
I can mix,
I can saw,
I can pour,
I can shift,
I can lift.
I'm clever, I'm smart,
And I listen lots too,
So I can be anything,
And so can you.

Zoo Keeper

I love animals,
Big and small,
I really like lions,
I'm not scared at all.
I would like to help feed them,
And brush their manes,
I would learn just how,
to keep them tame.
I want to be a zoo keeper
when I grow up.
I'm clever, I'm smart
And I listen lots too
So I can be anything,
And so can you.

Singer

My voice is blissful,
I love to sing.
To become a singer,
Would be the greatest thing.
I'd dress up nice,
I'd put on shows,
I might be famous one day,
Who knows?
I'm clever, I'm smart,
And I listen lots too,
So I can be anything,
And so can you.

Engineer

I like to discover,
I like to explore,
I like to know what's behind closed doors.
I like to figure,
And work things out,
I like to understand what things are about.
I want to be an engineer
when I grow up.
I'm clever, I'm smart,
And I listen lots too,
So I can be anything,
And so can you.

Ballerina

I'm skilfully graceful,
I'm daintily elegant,
Seamlessly gliding,
I feel magnificent.
I want to b e a ballerina some day
I'd dance my best in a theatre play.
I'm clever, I'm smart,
And I listen lots too,
So I can be anything,
And so can you.

Artist

I can draw lines,
I can draw circles,
I can use paints,
My favourite is purple.
Designing pictures is a fun thing to do,
My art is to share.
Between me and you,
I'm going to be an artist when I grow up.
I'm clever, I'm smart,
And I listen lots too,
So I can be anything,
And so can you

COOL
HAIR

Hairdresser

I love to style,
I love to curl,
I love to straighten,
I love to twirl.
I'd like to be a hairdresser,
I can wash your hair
or
Change the colour,
Whatever you need done it's no bother.
I'm clever, I'm smart,
And I listen lots too,
So I can be anything,
And so can you

Actor

I can change my voice,
I can make funny faces,
I can pretend I'm in different places.
I can roar like a lion,
I can bark like a pup,
I've got plenty of disguises.
I'm good at dressing up,
I'd like to be an actor when I grow up.
I'm clever, I'm smart,
And I listen lots too,
So I can be anything,
And so can you

Gardener

I would like to be a gardener,
Flowers are so pretty.
Daisies, roses,
Tulips and posies,
All smell good to me.
I enjoy cutting, pruning,
Planting seeds,
But I watch out for those pesky bees!
I'm clever, I'm smart,
And I listen lots too,
So I can be anything,
And so can you

Footballer

I would like to be a footballer,
I can run very fast,
I'm a good team player,
I know just how to pass.
I have very quick feet,
I can balance a ball on my nose,
I know how to score,
I get loads of goals.
I'm clever, I'm smart,
And I listen lots too,
So I can be anything,
And so can you.

Police Officer

I'm going to be a police officer one day
I will help,
I'll protect,
I will detect,
I'll inspect,
I will blow my whistle,
I will flash my badge,
I'll arrest all the robbers
And everyone that's bad.
I'm clever, I'm smart,
And I listen lots too,
So I can be anything,
And so can you.

Teacher

I am patient
I am kind,
I work with children,
I always make time.
I help them learn,
To read and write.
All my pupils are very bright,
I'm going to be a teacher some day.
I'm clever, I'm smart,
And I listen lots too
So I can be anything,
And so can you.

Astronaut

I would like to be an astronaut,
I'd take off into the air,
Bouncing on the moon,
Among the stars,
You'll find me there.
I'd travel the planets,
Pluto, Mars and any-other place.
And just before I return,
I'll explore the amazing space.
I'm clever, I'm smart,
And I listen lots too,
So I can be anything,
And so can you.

I Can Be Anything!

If I were taught that perhaps one day,

I could become whatever I may,

I'd certainly prove, by the thing that I'd choose,

That I can do, much more than you knew.

I am more than what you see.

What will I do? What can I be?

I think deep down, you'll be ever so pleased,

By what I can, one day achieve,

As I would decide to work very hard,

Stay up hours long,

And make perfectly sure, among the stars, I'll belong.

I'm clever, I'm smart,

And I listen lots too,

So I can be anything.

Help my dreams come true!

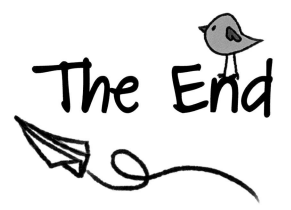